REUNITE ME WITH MY WITH MY BREATH ONCE AGAIN:

12 Breath of God

BY

KATHY BROCKS

Reunite me with my breath once again:
12 Breath of God
By
Kathy Brocks

Reunite me with my breath once again:
12 Breath of God
By
Kathy Brocks

ISBN: 978-0-615-15798-6
Copyright © 2008
Revised 2010
All Rights Reserved
kathyabrocks@
gmail.com
P.O. Box 353
Elgin, IL 60121

SPECIAL PREFACE

I often believed God missed the intimacy of us, his creation.
The gift of salvation to be reunited with the father again

Talking with God can be fun.   Like Jesus he has a sense of humor
God wants to hear from us.   He said in his word speak what you want and sent his son to do everything through speaking.   Jesus could have used other ways to accomplish the Father's will but God wants to know what is in your heart.   The best way to know this is by what spills forth from your mouth.   He does not want to force anything on you.   God wants you to choose, they way He made a choice to choose us, saves us.

It is like new parents that want their baby's first word to be, "Mommy or Daddy".
That first connection of communication is the best sound you can hear because it tells you that this little person knows who I am and will never forget me.

God wants to know that we know who he is and what he means to us.
God believes we were worth the sacrifice and would do it all over again because he loves us

more than we can imagine.   God wants to
hear about our good days and bad days.   God
wants us to know He has already provided for
every conceivable need we will have no matter
the twists and turns we take throughout our
life.

When we call out to Him and accept Christ as
our lord and savior I imagine God saying
"Yes!" you know my NAME!   He hugs and
lifts you up in the spirit.
Reuniting with the breath of God once again

Table of Contents

Reunite me with my breath once again!

12 breath of God
Reference: Matt 5:3 God blesses those who realize
their need for him, for the Kingdom of Heaven is
given to them

Breath One
"My Son for you"

Take in my sweet smelling scent
You cannot exhale me you can only take me in
Take in my sweet aroma
To know Me is to Love Me
To be like Me is to have my nature
To have Me is to truly truly accept my Son,
The one who volunteered His life for yours
My Son, the only link to heaven and earth
My Son, the only one to move through the pits of hell
with full authority

Another option, yes
My Son, offered to share His house with you,
To fight your battle, to take back the authority you
gave away so freely,
So he could get to know you intimately, he wants to
fellowship with you

I love my Son.   Because I love my Son, I allowed it,
I forgave you
To be My creation is to have my breath flowing
through your lungs.
To love is to know I am separated from My breath

because of one man's choice.
To come home again is to be alive through the blood
of my Son

Let Me see you through my Son
Without my Son I do not even recognize the breath in
you
Allow me to take you into the swirls of my breath
And when you go through battles your breath will be
victorious
Allow me to take you into the swirls of My breath
And when sin invites you to take a seat
You will rebuke it without hesitation

I have a glorious solution for all your woes
My Son

Breath One
"My Son for you"
Scripture Association

John 3:16

For God so loved the world, that he gave his only
begotten Son,
that whosoever believeth in him should not
perish but have everlasting life

Genesis 2:4-7

This is the account of the creation of the heavens
and the earth.
When God made the heavens and the earth, there
were no plants
or grain growing on   the earth, for the Lord God
had not sent any rain.
And no one was there to cultivate the soil.   But
water came up out of the ground and
watered all the land.   And the Lord God formed
a man's body from the dust of the ground
and breathed into it the breath of life.   And the
living Man became a living person.

Breath Two
"Believe"

Shut up already! Deg!
You never stop your yammering
I wish I had this, I wish I had that
Consider me, include me
"I ain't got know money"
Lives in the catacombs of your mind

Hey! We use to be cool
Sitting in the cut watching everybody go by
Then you upped and left me in the shadows
Now I'm tooting my soda laughing at you
In your fancy golden arch uniform
I believed we'd always stay the same
Same wants, same don'ts
You said conformity's for the birds

So now you want to prosper
Believe without murmuring
Your life feels constipated
You want a house, wealth, family go get it
Stop signifying at God's people, He didn't block
you
I should have, I wish I did,
So and so lied to me, cheated me
Forgive and move on
Call for your stuff
It's laid up in a storage bin in heaven

Breath Two
"Believe"
Scripture Association

Mark 11:22-24

"Have faith in God.   I assure you that you can say to this mountain, 'May God lift you and throw you into the sea,' and your command will be obeyed.   All that's required is that you really believe and do not doubt in your heart.   Listen to me!   You can pray for anything, and if you believe, you will have it.   But when you are praying first forgive anyone you are holding a grudge against, so that your Father in heaven will forgive your sins, too."

Breath Three
"See Me in your eyes"

I look into your eyes and see no flame
Where is the fire; the light that beams
The light that ignites the radio waves, pulling in
the bench warmers,
The next greats, the diligent, the slacker, the
thief, the faithful drunk
For pious work is to be done

How hot does your fire burn
Hot enough to hold treasures, to burn off the
limbs of your enemy
Rev it up, complacency has you bound

You hater of the unwashed
I can't see myself in the mirrors of your eyes for
the dew of the many mirrors of you

How the blind fails to see
I am the Flame, stamped out with credulous
pedestals
Throw off your diamonds, jewels and fancy
clothes; pursue Me with fervor
Seek My fire with thrusted blows

Till smoke of the fire that burns, taunts My
nostrils

Singeing hairs beyond My grasp

Perfected grace, love rolling out of the mouth of
man sweetens the palate
Hallelujah, I can see the image of Me in the
center of your eyes

<u>Breath Three</u>
"See Me in your eyes"

Scripture Association

John 6:41-42

"And why worry about a speck in your friend's
eye when you have a log in your own?   How
can you think of saying, 'Friend, let me help you
get rid of that speck in your eye, 'when you can't
see past the log from your own eye?   Hypocrite!
First get rid of the log from your own eye; then
perhaps you will see well enough to deal with the
speck in your friend's eye.

Breath Four
"Moderation Speak"

Moderation
Moderation is the golden ring
Slimmer waist, moderation
Cuter face, moderation
Size 6, moderation
How moderate we inner city, outer city folks
must be
Standing in the welfare lines, taking double shifts
at fast food joints
Doing the corporate glide and working at the toy
store on the side
Moderation, takes on many forms, duress, just to
name one
Holes in your draws
Shoes flapping and talking more than you do
Moderation, the excess of poverty

Hold back,
How do you work out moderation when you
don't have enough?
Moderation, no money for food for the week

He said you could go into the store and buy food
and clothes without money
I can get with that kind of moderation, abundance
that is

Say what you want and it's yours appearing
before your face
The Water Walker said it and did it with grace

What's the difference did we loose our
connection
Or has moderation permeated the depth of our
soul reserved for Him

When did we stop talking to Him?
He's standing in front of us holding mounds of
clothes and food
But we keep walking passed Him
Money, shoes, houses, limbs, inventions,
husbands, wives
Thumped your head yet?

Breath Four
Scripture Association

"Moderation Speak"

1 Peter 1:3-6

All honor to the God and Father of our Lord
Jesus Christ, for it is by his boundless mercy that
God has given us the privilege of being born
again.   Now we live with a wonderful
expectation because Jesus Christ rose again from
the dead.   4. For God has reserved a priceless
inheritance for his children.   It is kept in heaven
for you, pure and undefiled, beyond the reach of
change and decay. 5. And God, in his mighty
power, will protect you until you receive this
salvation, because you are   trusting him.   It will
be revealed on the last day for all to see.   6. So
be truly glad!   There is wonderful joy ahead,
even though it is necessary for you to endure
many trials for a while.

Breath Five
"Do you Hear Me"

I strain my heart with every word to hear your
voice
Seven years I cried aloud "open the doors"
I wait in silence for the solution
With every cent I gladly give you first
Grinding I go to and fro with only weekly
whispers of work
You I give my last cause you said you'd always
provide more
With ignorant joy I believe, I speak what you say
A few bumps along the way
Then I hear you say, "What do you want?"
  Unsure its you I have nothing to say
"Oh, wait don't leave, just keep things from
getting worse"
"This you say after all the years of prayer
To this is yours, one who has no want of
anything"

<u>Breath Five</u>
Scripture Association
"Do you hear me?"

2 Chronicles 7:14-16

Then if my people who are called by my name
will humble themselves and pray and seek my
face and turn from their wicked ways, I will hear
from heaven and will forgive their sins and heal
their land. 15. I will listen to every sin prayer
made in this place, 16. for I have chosen this
Temple and set it apart to be my home forever.
My eyes and heart will always be here.

Breath Six
"Woman in Red"

Even though you are not a man, Job, I shall call
you
Rich in spirit love and grace
Mercy beyond that I have seen in the days I
looked upon you all
Loyal to me without fault you stand,
Down dark streets you go to worship Me
Wait on corners for buses with bullets flying by
prostitutes, drugs and murderers see you from a
far
with harm in their hearts they approach; you
smile; to you they say "hi sister, how's it going
miss lady"; My glory surrounds you
with some you share the Word and others you
invite to church

Animals I've called to walk on all fours you're
called just for loving Me
And still you stand refusing to curse Me or hate
them
On your spirit they try to latch, to Me you call
with authority
Poor in spirit
That's not you
To no man you bow

To Me you surrender all
I love more than you can utter, more than you
know
Because even scared you chose Me
Your God I am, my child you are dressed in the
blood of My Son
Because I love you I made clothing from His
blood and a non-removable zipper of gold
Put shoes upon your feet
Your head and hands uncovered
To and fro you may go just like my Son.
The battle that remains is what you choose
The mind so vast
Just know I am always with you

Breath Six
"Woman in Red"
Scripture Association

Matthew 26:28-29

for this is my blood, which seals the covenant
between God and his people.   It is poured out to
forgive the sins of many.   29. Mark my
words—I will not drink wine again until the day I
drink it new with you in my Father's Kingdom.

Breath Seven
"Light"

Oh light of heaven rain down on me
Loosen the ring of torment that encapsulate my
body
Make free an arm I can raise as a sign of praise
Let my legs move at my will
Wrists steady to lift my own weight
Oh light of heaven rain down on me

New eyes I can see smooth new skin free of
grease burns
And belt marks, skid marks of fingernails fade
my hairless epidermis
To see the regret of wrong turns on my tattered
feet
Cute short hair not enough to draw in the gaze of
scattered love
Oh light of heaven rain down on me

I hear the wind on the blows that stole the birds'
chirp at my window ceil
Lusts' tip that rolled around in my ear
No promise of the next hour, definitely no
tomorrow
Wisdom of no age, just unloved, not coached
Before baby and me, bid I not be, two opposites,
bitter sweet
Lift the confusion of it all
Oh light of heaven rain down on me

A city on a hill can not be hidden
Obscurity has no vale
Arrows pointed at my heart
Fellows gorge my unrest
Pungent aroma fills my breath
A glimmer stands in the back of my mind
Smoke of incense fills the halls
A name I am, one you call
Oh light of God ran down on me

<u>Breath Seven</u>
Scripture Association
"Light"

John 8:12

Jesus said to the people, "I am the light of the
world.   If you follow me, you won't be
stumbling through the darkness, because you will
have the light that leads to life."

2 Corinthians 4: 6-18

For God, who said, "Let there be light in the
darkness," has made us understand that this light
is the brightness of the glory of God that is seen
in the face of Jesus Christ.   7.   But this precious
treasure—this light and power that now shine
within us—is held in perishable containers, that
is, in our weak bodies.   So everyone can see that
our glorious power if from God and is not our
own.   8.   We are pressed on every side by
troubles, but we are not crushed and broken.   We
are perplexed, but we don't give up and quit. 9.
We are hunted down but God never abandoned
us.   We get knocked down but we get up again
and keep going.   16b.Though our bodies are
dying, our spirits are being renewed every day.

Breath Eight
"Salt"
(Thank you for coming into the lives of a tri-fold
field of wounded women and loved them
completely-Thank you)

Brother not of skin
Beloved man
Road warrior
Finder of treasures
Lifter of ravaged packages
Son of God, Man after His heart, you are
Waterer of wilted lilies
Mender of broken bridges

Hold tight tears roll down, soaking clinched fists
You are for a time such as this
Water walker, no feat to great to achieve
Speaking spirit-say it, say it again
I am rejuvenated daily
No burden so heavy that God has not already
overcome
I am the son of God, he knows me and I know
Him
He is my Father and I love Him always
I walk in the strength of your Love Lord
I will walk the waters,
I will say what you say,
I am, I will, forever love her
Father your will in me, I in you, we will love
them all

Breath Eight
"Salt"
Scripture Association

Mark 9:49-50

For everyone will be purified with fire.   Salt is good for seasoning.   But if it loses its flavor, how do you make it salty again? You must have the qualities of salt among yourselves and live in peace with each other.

Breath Nine
"Secrets"

It isn't every day I let someone see the inside of
me
It isn't everyday I let you inside
Letting you inside is a reward I reserve for
special occasions
Like the marriage of best friends, the birth of a
baby, the death of a son
It isn't every day I let someone see the inside of
me
Like lips on the inside of a honeydew
Closer to you I want to be
To see the heave of your chest
Tears stroking your cheeks
  Sun bouncing off your hair
To you a rose I dare
Gaze upon your beauty
Lavender's pungent stain has no hold for my
bravado
Breast of fireballs, with hollowed nads I stroll
To tame the beast of old
There's no certain thing
I do what most do
In my mind I design bracelets of diamonds and
rubies
I string together poems and songs
I imagine the day money will rain from heaven
Imagine one of my stories made into a movie

wiping the dirty car oil from my knuckles
and sweat from my brow I resign to the daily
grind, pursuit of lusciousness
so firm quarters drop at his feet
babe for now, who?, the next hour
nullify my taste for salty hips
the harder I try the farther I fall
Fear says letting you on the inside of me does no
great damage at all
Show me beauty I can't hold
Tell me things I can't see in my dreams
Be real with me and you can strip the roots of my
pleasured pain
Let me on the inside

Breath Nine
Scriptures Secrets
"Secrets"

That is why we have a great High Priest who has
gone to Heaven, Jesus the Son of God. Let us
cling to him and never stop trusting him. This
High Priest of ours understands our
Weaknesses, for he faced all of the same
temptations we do, yet he did not sin. So let us
come boldly to the throne of our gracious God.
There we will receive his mercy, and we will find
grace to help us when we need it.

Scripture Association

Hebrews 4:14-16

Seeing then that we have a great high priest, that
is passed into the heavens, Jesus the Son of God,
let us hold fast our profession. For we have not
an high priest, which can not be touched with the
feeling of our infirmities; but was in all points
tempted like as we are, yet without sin. Let us
therefore come boldly unto the throne of grace,
that we may obtain mercy, and find grace to help
in time of need.

Breath Ten
"Trespasses"

Illegal in every way he came at me with mighty
blows
Like a kitten trapped in a pipe with a barking
Doberman on each end
There I coward in the center of the bed begging
God for an end
To no avail there they came one by one
High five in and high five out
Some strapped down
Others loosed
No form, no grace
There I was a piñata with no face
One more till my next fix
"Babe" he whispered, like he knew my name
"Shoot I couldn't remember it"
Tracks on my arms and tracks on my legs
Staggering I made my way down the hall
To my baby's crib, there I laid body tender with a
needle hanging from my face
Drifting into a deep sleep while the harmonic
cries of my new baby flows on and on
She's only been here a week

Breath Ten
"Trespasses "

Scripture Association

Psalm 69:1-3

Save me, O God,
For the floodwaters are up to my neck
Deeper and deeper I sink into the mire;
I can't find a foothold to stand on
I am in deep water, and the floods overwhelm me
I am exhausted from crying for help; my throat is
parched and dry
My eyes are swollen with weeping, waiting for
my God to help me.

Breath Eleven
"Water Walker"

Ride my ten speed across Lake Michigan I will
Defy gravity on the highest hill
In a room without doors I am
Melt the ice surrounding broken hearts
If breaking wind is all it takes to escape
There I am in the mist holding your right cheek
Long summer days and short winter nights
Defying gravity on my ten speed bike
Cross country to prove love's still here
A dollar per mile, away I am on to the next town
New limbs from few words and no touch
Spot the moon on the brightest of days and
darkest of nights
I ride the waves on my ten speed bike, over
Africa and Asia Minor
There I am with dirty hands and a free conscious
To my father with love I do it all, no toiling for
me with joy I go
On my ten speed bike snatching souls from
deaths' choke hold
Tomorrow a possibility never guaranteed it
doesn't take a bus or a bullet to take you out
A pill, a minute of passion, liquor is enough to let
the smoke of slow rot into your house
If you want to ride across Lake Michigan with
me on your ten speed bike
Whisper my name, "Jesus" and I'll hear and bid
you to ride with me on your ten speed bike

Breath Eleven
"Water Walker"
Scripture Association
Matthew 14:22-31

And straightway Jesus constrained his disciples
to get into a ship, and to go before him unto the
other side, while he sent the multitudes away.
And when he had sent the multitudes away, he
went up into a mountain apart to pray: and when
the evening was come, he was there alone
But the ship was now in the midst of the sea,
tossed with waves: for the wind was contrary
And in the forth watch of the night Jesus went
unto them, walking on the sea
And when the disciples saw him walking on the
sea, they were troubled, saying, it is a spirit: and
they cried out for fear
But straightway Jesus spake unto them, saying,
"Be of good cheer; it is I; be not afraid"
And Peter answered him and said, Lord if it be
thou, bid me come unto thee on the water
And he said, "Come" and when Peter was come
down out of the ship, he walked on the water to
go to Jesus

But when he saw the wind boisterous, he was afraid; and beginning to sink, he cried out, saying, Lord, save me
And immediately Jesus stretched forth his hand, and caught him, and said unto him,
" O thou of little faith, wherefore didst thou doubt?"
And when they were come into the ship, the wind ceased.

Breath Twelve
"Not for Sale"

12 years old, 10 0'clock on a Friday night
Bladder full; crusty eyes open

I remember thinking I wish I had some decent
clothes to wear.
When this thought came across my mind.   I
knew it wrong.

What for the first time I ever felt like my core
said, "No"!
But I said it anyway, "I'll sell my soul for some
clothes", the Spiegel's ad from last Sunday's
Times was sprawled on the bathroom floor.
A pink corduroy pant and jacket and other stuff, I
really wanted every thing on
the page.   I was tired of looking like a rag doll.
We lived in a middle class neighborhood but
dress like we lived in the projects or something, I
didn't know until folks told me and then I hated
it.   I even told the devil to put them in my
dresser draw.

When I said it remorse came over me and I knew
that was a mistake and really didn't want to go to
hell.   But had no clue what to do next. It still did
not seem real to me.   I had no idea of what it was
but suddenly I clearly understood it was not
where I was to be at all.   Not even close.

I went to bed.

Later that night about midnight I was awakened

There was a light shining out of my draw.   A voice was calling me.

I turned to look, stood up and decided, "My soul is more valuable than clothes".

I got back in bed and didn't think about it again and never asked my mom for clothes or anything for myself

I just accepted whatever God provided.

A month later she came home with some pink, green and blue blouses.

Breath Twelve

"Not for Sale"

Scripture Association

Gen 2:6-7
And the Lord God formed man of the dust of the
ground, and breathed into his nostrils the breath
of life; and man became a living soul.

Gen 1:26
Then God said let us make man in our image
after our likeness: and let then have dominion
over the fish of the sea, and over the fowl of the
air, and over the cattle, and over all the earth, and
over every creeping thing that creep upon the
earth

Closing Words

If you can identify with one of these poems, a part, phrase, word or if you know you need someone bigger, stronger and more love than you can ever give, invite Jesus Christ into your life now.   Tomorrow truly is not promised.

All the things you hear preachers and other Christians tell you is true; you can put down this book and die the next minute and spend an eternity in hell.   It's not the flesh that will be tortured it's your soul, your mind, the place where memories hide.   Think of your soul as a memory board, a computer.   The torture comes when all the times the gift of salvation was offered and you declined.   Every awful moment you ever experienced times a million.

Remember when you wanted to go somewhere your family was or friends were but you were not allowed?   If you die and go to hell, you will want to get out.   It's the same with the Kingdom of Heaven; you'll want to get in.   Christ is the only way into the Kingdom of Heaven, where God reigns.   Every good place requires a passkey.   Christ is the passkey to Heaven.

Now you can doubt and test it out for yourself. This passage will play over and over in your head. Or you can give Jesus a chance to show your pure love.　When you walk with God if you allow him he will take away your pain.　And when you get to heaven you will forget the things of earth and revel in the things of the Kingdom. Choose now pure love, everlasting joy or a constant reminder of every hurtful thing you've done or experienced.

If your decision is Jesus Christ, the son of God repeat this confession.

Prayer confession
Great decision!
Read aloud.

Lord, I know I am a sinner
I know I can't earn or buy my way into heaven
I want to know your pure love
Lord I freely accept Jesus as my Savior and Lord
of my life
From this day forward I give my life to you Jesus
Direct me in all my ways and keep me on your
path
Set me in an atmosphere of learning in a bible
based church
In your name Jesus, thank you

Rules of the (Christian) Road

At first it seems rather hard to stay in the mainstream of Christianity. To be more than just a good Christian is the goal of the majority of Christians. It's what can I do or how can I help attitude.   However the goal is to stay on this road but act in the same place as yesterday. So, what can we as Christians do to move ahead in our walk? There are several things. But before we do anything we've got to go to God and prostrate ourselves, you know, pray.

to you through the shed blood of your son, Jesus. Second, praise him and exalt his name for without God true worth and eternal happiness is absolutely unattainable. Third, since 90% of prayer is petition bring fourth your petitions.

Ask God for everything that is in your heart and if you just don't know what to ask for call on   the Holy Spirit of God to intercede on your behalf. And even if you know what you want to do to be a blessing to the church but don't know how to go about it, pray. Ask God for guidance and then begin to act on that prayer. You can go to your Cell Leader or Pastor and tell them of your desire and they will assist you. Sometimes the areas in which we desire to work have yet to be established or are in the making.   If it's in the process then ask if you can assist with the process. However, if it doesn't exist then create it, with the permission of the Pastor.

WAIT! You say   Start it, ask for help. I just got saved. I don't even know what I'm doing. All I know is that I get up and comb my hair every morning and hope I don't end up dead on some street corner. I answered the alter call because what the preacher was saying seemed better than how I was living. I just got tired of being afraid. Now, all I have is just another fear. It's different but it's still a fear. I fear failing at this new job as a Christian. It's is a job right just like anything else I have to work at it. I don't feel equipped.

These concerns are so real. Everybody feels this way whether they are new to Christ, a backslider and sometimes those that have walked with Christ for all of their lives. However the latter is not to scare you but is sometimes just a fact. It's partly being attacked by Satan and just not being equipped from the beginning.

When a person first gives themselves to God it's like walking through a smoke filled room and exhaling at the clearing or just knowing it's okay to jump off of the teeter totter. You stand alone at the alter but you feel as though you've just married an entire clan. You're all excited you don't know what to do first, should you tell your best friend, tell your mom. You've got to tell someone you feel like you're going to burst.   So, you run outside and scream to the world, "I'm free!!!!!!!! I'm free!!!!! Thank you Jesus! I'm free!"

Now as the police at concerts say, "It's time for crowd control". You need to be taught to scream your salvation in more than just belching it out to the world. The after taste should last longer than a two minute song. This is where the soul warriors come into play. "Soul Warriors" are Christ's soldiers, children of God, winners of souls for Christ, your brothers and sisters in Christ, what they do is win souls for Christ first and then maintain and build up or edify you so that you may know the truth and trust in God always and for all things just as Jesus did. The goal is to be like Jesus, to be a citizen of the kingdom of God and to get you where Jesus is now.   The veterans or soul warriors minister to you just as the Lord did to Jesus and Jesus to his disciples and they did to each other. You are taken in under the wings of a brother or sister in Christ and he, she or they will teach you how to live a Christian life.   No, you won't be in a commune. Where you live is your decision.   But, you will have to make some changes in your daily life. No, you shouldn't be asked to give away all of your money. God only required 10% of your gross income, which is called tithing. Tithes are used to maintain the church. The Pastor's salary comes from this, the utilities, advertising, blessings to help those less fortunate.

The brethren will answer any questions you may have regarding the word of God, the Bible. Yes, you will be asked to read your bible. Not everyone starts out reading the bible daily but it helps. Reading the word of God is a vital tool used in prayer. Knowing the word of God strengthens your knowledge of God, and increases your prayer ability. Simply put, you have more to pray about. In the word it illustrates how God not only desires fervent prayer but God also requires variety. And variety comes through the knowledge of God and knowledge through reading the word of God.

"Rules of the (Christian) road"

Prayer

Romans 8:26

In the same way, the spirit helps us in our
weakness.   We do not know what we ought to
pray for, but the spirit himself intercedes for us
with groans that words can not express

The "Five finger" prayer method; spend five
minutes on each finger this should get you to
25-30 minutes prayer length. Each day increase
each finger by five minutes.   There is no real
limit this is to get you to pray for at least an hour.

1st – Thumb Since this is the closest to you it is
for friends, family, neighbors.
2nd – Index Pray for those that guide or teach
you; your mentors, Pastor, Church leaders etc

3rd - Middle Finger Is for governmental leaders, people in authority

4th - Fourth or Ring Finger is for the sick, homeless etc.

5th- Pinky Finger Pray for Yourself

Prayer is speaking to God.   You are speaking to a higher being, higher than man. When we pray we are showing our need for God.   You get restoration wisdom, healing, overcome the devil and meets needs through prayer.

First acknowledge God by meditating on God. Second, anticipate God being with you. Third, come with desire .have a deep longing to speak with God. Fourth, pray with fervency.

<u>Notes</u>

NOTES

Author Page
Email:kathyabrocks@gmail.com

I am a Christian.   I believe Jesus Christ is Lord.   I believe in the Father, Son and Holy Ghost.   I do respect other faiths.   It is always interesting to learn other's faith.   No matter your faith I hope you enjoy reading and rereading my collection of poetry.   Write your opinions on my page at lulu.com